Earth Under Construction!
VOLCANOES
RESHAPE EARTH!

BY CHARLIE LIGHT

Gareth Stevens
PUBLISHING

Please visit our website, www.garethstevens.com. For a free color catalog of all our high-quality books, call toll free 1-800-542-2595 or fax 1-877-542-2596.

Cataloging-in-Publication Data

Names: Light, Charlie.
Title: Volcanoes reshape Earth! / Charlie Light.
Description: New York : Gareth Stevens Publishing, 2021. | Series: Earth under construction! | Includes glossary and index.
Identifiers: ISBN 9781538258347 (pbk.) | ISBN 9781538258361 (library bound) | ISBN 9781538258354 (6 pack)
Subjects: LCSH: Volcanoes–Juvenile literature.
Classification: LCC QE522.L54 2021 | DDC 551.21–dc23

First Edition

Published in 2021 by
Gareth Stevens Publishing
111 East 14th Street, Suite 349
New York, NY 10003

Copyright © 2021 Gareth Stevens Publishing

Designer: Sarah Liddell
Editor: Kate Mikoley

Photo credits: Cover, p. 1 Wead/Shutterstock.com; space background and Earth image used throughout Aphelleon/Shutterstock.com; caution tape used throughout Red sun design/Shutterstock.com; p. 5 MARK GARLICK/SCIENCE PHOTO LIBRARY/Science Photo Library/Getty Images; p. 7 Digital Vision/DigitalVision/Getty Images; p. 9 Langevin Jacques/Contributor/Sygma/Getty Images; p. 11 Designua/Shutterstock.com; p 13 (top) DrNegative/Wikimedia Commons; p. 13 (bottom) Roman Khomlyak/Shutterstock.com; p. 15 Pung/Shutterstock.com; p. 17 FERDI AWED/Contributor/AFP/Getty images; p. 19 BardoczPeter/iStock/Getty Images Plus/Getty Images; p. 21 Dhoxax/E+/Getty Images; p. 23 Irosebrugh/iStock/Getty Images Plus/Getty Images; p. 25 Hans Strand/Corbis Documentary/Getty Images; p. 27 Smith Collection/Gado/Contributor/Archive Photos/Getty Images; p. 29 Anadolu Agency/Contributor/Anadolu Agency/Getty Images.

All rights reserved. No part of this book may be reproduced in any form without permission in writing from the publisher, except by a reviewer.

Printed in the United States of America

Some of the images in this book illustrate individuals who are models. The depictions do not imply actual situations or events.

CPSIA compliance Information: Batch #CS20GS: For further information contact Gareth Stevens, New York, New York at 1-800-542-2595.

CONTENTS

Earth's Explosive Changes 4
Predicting Volcanoes 6
Violent Volcanoes 8
Stratovolcanoes 10
Mount Saint Helens 12
Caldera Volcanoes 14
Krakatau Erupts 16
Submarine Volcanoes 18
Shield Volcanoes 20
Lava Domes 22
Fissures and Fields 24
Supervolcanoes 26
Recent Eruptions 28
Glossary 30
For More Information 31
Index 32

Words in the glossary appear in **bold** type the first time they are used in the text.

EARTH'S EXPLOSIVE CHANGES

Volcanoes are part of our changing planet. They're openings in Earth's crust. Magma, gas, and ash from inside Earth come out of these openings. Magma is very hot rock under Earth's surface. The rock is so hot that it's molten, or melted to a liquid. Magma rises up through cracks in the solid rock around it. It fills up openings in the rock called magma chambers. Finally, it erupts out of volcanoes! When magma reaches the surface, it's called lava.

Volcanic eruptions can be slow and runny when the magma is thin. But when the magma is very thick, it can erupt in an explosion!

THERE ARE MORE THAN 450 VOLCANOES IN THE RING OF FIRE. NINETY PERCENT OF **EARTHQUAKES** HAPPEN IN THE RING TOO!

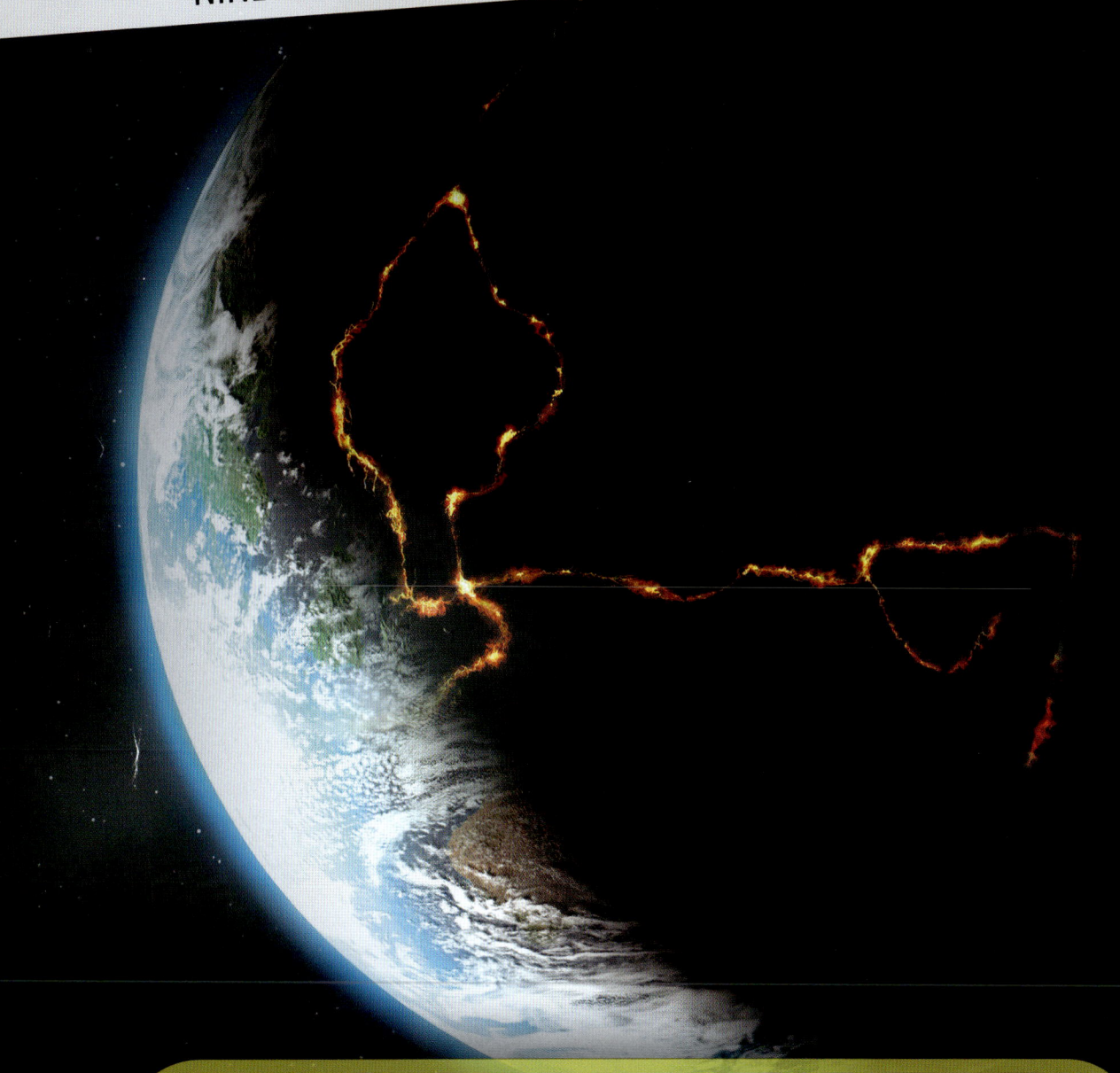

RING OF FIRE

Earth's crust is made up of big chunks called tectonic plates. When the plates bump, they can cause earthquakes and volcanoes and make mountains. Seventy-five percent of Earth's volcanoes are in a place in the Pacific Ocean where tectonic plates meet. It's called the Ring of Fire.

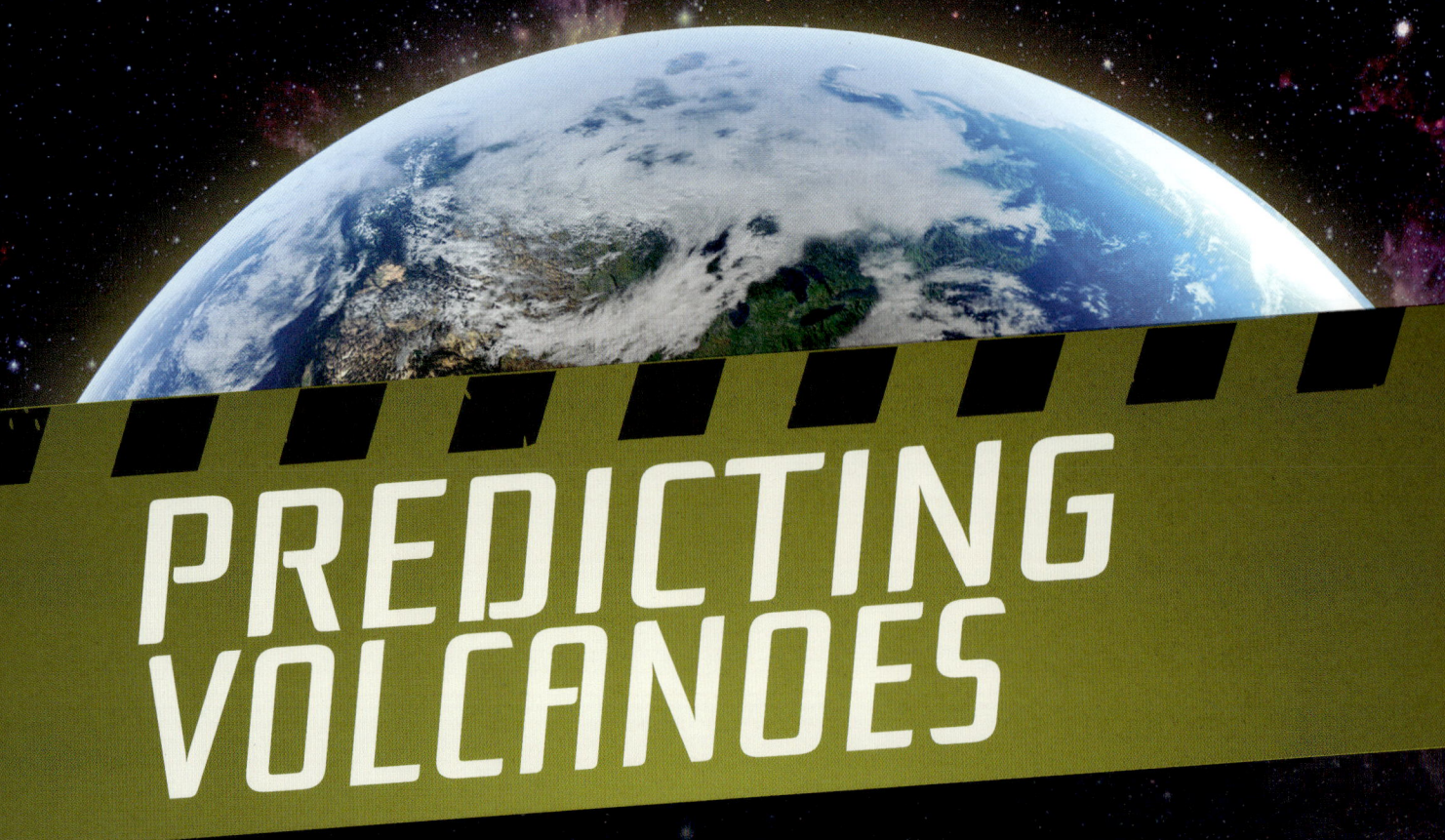

PREDICTING VOLCANOES

Scientists who study volcanoes are called volcanologists. They watch for signs that a volcano is going to erupt. Earthquakes are a big sign. Magma rising up can shake the ground. Earthquakes can get stronger and happen more often before an eruption.

Volcanologists use **satellites** to measure changes inside the volcano. Rocks in the magma chamber can crack before an eruption. Gas can start leaking out of the volcano. Gas can also make the ground swell before an eruption. Tools called tiltmeters measure changes to a volcano's slope. All these measurements are called data. Today, special computers use data to **predict** eruptions!

ABOUT ONE OUT OF 20 PEOPLE LIVE WITHIN DANGEROUS DISTANCE OF AN ACTIVE VOLCANO. VOLCANOLOGISTS TELL PEOPLE WHEN THEY NEED TO EVACUATE, OR LEAVE QUICKLY, BEFORE AN ERUPTION.

VOLCANOES CAN GO EXTINCT?

Volcanologists call volcanoes active, dormant, or extinct. A volcano that has erupted since the last ice age (about 10,000 years ago) is active. A dormant volcano hasn't erupted since the last ice age, but could erupt again. A volcano is extinct when volcanologists believe it will never erupt again.

VIOLENT VOLCANOES

Volcanic eruptions send out gas, ash, and lava. Gas can make it hard to breathe. Ash piling on buildings can make them fall. Lava usually moves slow enough for people to get away. It can still destroy roads, buildings, and plants. This can cause **famine**.

Pyroclastic flows are a mix of gas and hot rock. They move up to about 100 miles (161 km) per hour! Lahars are mudflows made up of volcanic matter mixed with water, mud, and **debris**. Both flows can kill people and animals.

Some volcanoes explode when they erupt, shooting out rocks, gas, lava, and ash. This can break the volcano apart.

IN 1985, THE NEVADO DEL RUIZ VOLCANO NEAR ARMERO, COLOMBIA, SET OFF A DEADLY LAHAR. IT KILLED ABOUT 23,000 PEOPLE.

VOLCANOES CAN CHANGE THE WEATHER!

Volcanoes can change Earth's weather and climate. Volcanic eruptions send gas into the air. Sunlight bounces off of some of these gases instead of reaching Earth. This makes the climate cooler. Other gases trap heat in the air, warming the planet. This is called the **greenhouse effect**.

STRATOVOLCANOES

Stratovolcanoes are some of the most serious volcanoes. They can have explosive eruptions. Stratovolcanoes are mountains made of layers of lava from past eruptions. When lava cools, it becomes hard. The layers are also made of tephra. This is rock and dust that erupts from a volcano.

Stratovolcanoes are shaped like cones. They're narrow and steep at the top and wide at the bottom. The tallest part of a volcano is called the summit. Stratovolcanoes have craters at their summits. A crater is a bowl-shaped hole. Eruptions come out of the crater. Sometimes, eruptions come out of vents, or openings, in the sides too.

INSIDE A STRATOVOLCANO

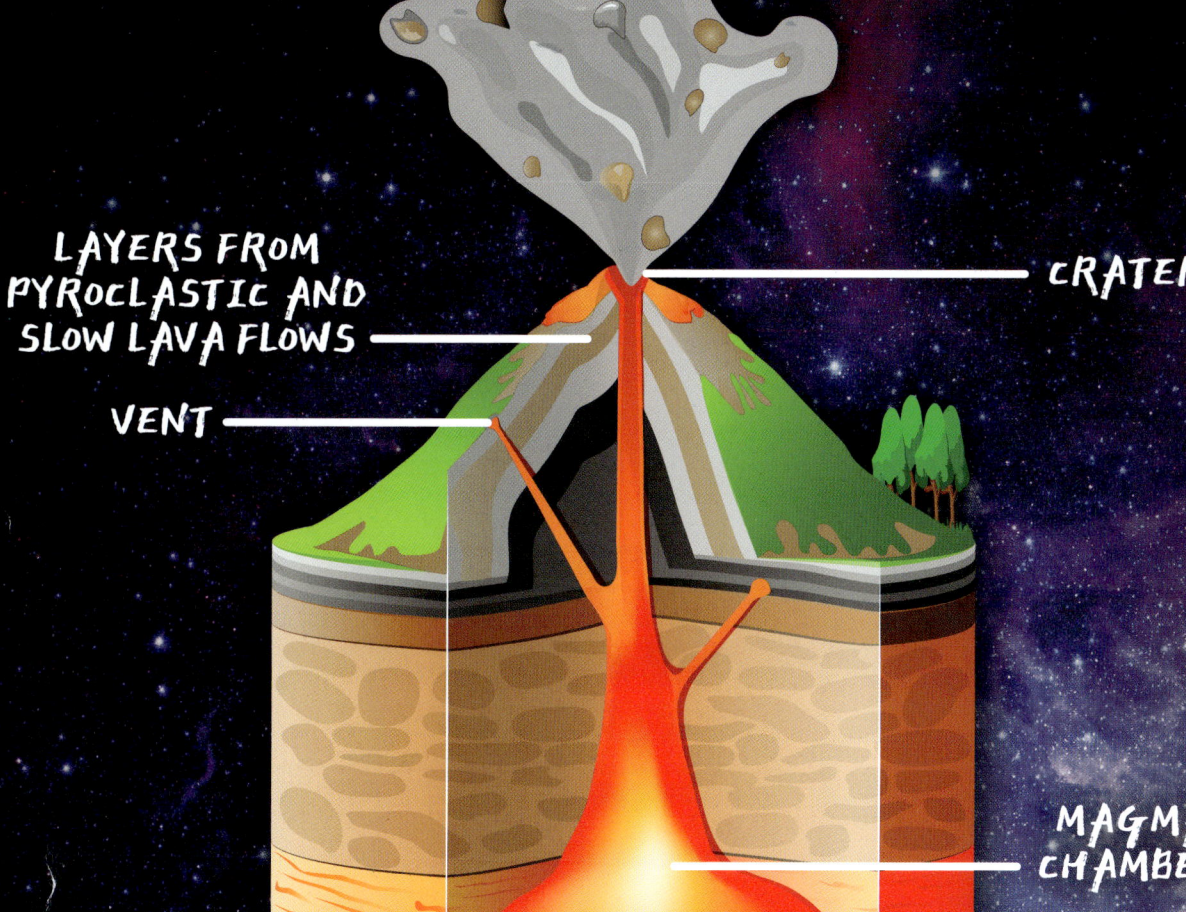

- LAYERS FROM PYROCLASTIC AND SLOW LAVA FLOWS
- VENT
- CRATER
- MAGMA CHAMBER

VOLCANOES CAN BUILD MOUNTAINS! THE VOLCANO IS THE OPENING IN THE CRUST. THE MOUNTAIN IS BUILT FROM THE LAVA AND ROCKS THAT ERUPT FROM THIS OPENING.

MOUNT VESUVIUS

Mount Vesuvius is one of the most famous stratovolcanoes. It's erupted more than 50 times! These eruptions usually have explosions and pyroclastic flows. The most famous eruption was in 79 CE. It destroyed two cities nearby called Pompeii and Herculaneum. Thousands of people were killed in the eruption.

MOUNT SAINT HELENS

Mount Saint Helens is one of the most famous stratovolcanoes. It's in the state of Washington. Its eruption in 1980 caused more harm than any other in U.S. history. Smaller earthquakes happened for months before the big eruption. Mount Saint Helens also let out steam.

Then on May 18, an earthquake hit the volcano. It knocked down part of the mountain! This caused the largest **landslide** ever recorded. It also set off a volcanic eruption. The eruption was so hot that it melted glaciers close by. The water mixed with debris from the eruption. This made a powerful lahar.

MOUNT SAINT HELENS BEFORE

THE MOUNT SAINT HELENS ERUPTION KILLED 57 PEOPLE AND THOUSANDS OF ANIMALS. TODAY, NATURE AROUND THE VOLCANO IS GROWING AGAIN.

MOUNT SAINT HELENS AFTER

AN EXPLOSIVE CHANGE

The 1980 eruption changed the whole area—and Mount Saint Helens itself. The top 1,300 feet (396 m) of the mountain **collapsed**. A U-shaped crater was left at the summit of the mountain. It grew to be about 1,300 feet (396 m) wide. The youngest glacier in North America rests inside the crater.

CALDERA VOLCANOES

Calderas are volcanic craters that are more than 0.6 mile (1 km) wide. Calderas are often bigger than craters, which are circular and formed mainly by exploding rock during eruptions. Most calderas start out as cone-shaped volcanoes. The magma chamber holding up the volcano collapses. This is usually from a big eruption. Then the summit of the cone falls and a huge crater is left behind.

Calderas can keep erupting after they form. Sometimes, these eruptions form new cone-shaped volcanoes inside the caldera. Lakes can also form inside these craters. Crater Lake in Oregon sits in a caldera that formed 7,700 years ago!

MOUNT MAZAMA FORMED THE CALDERA WHERE CRATER LAKE SITS TODAY. ITS POWERFUL ERUPTION MADE A BEAUTIFUL NEW LANDSCAPE.

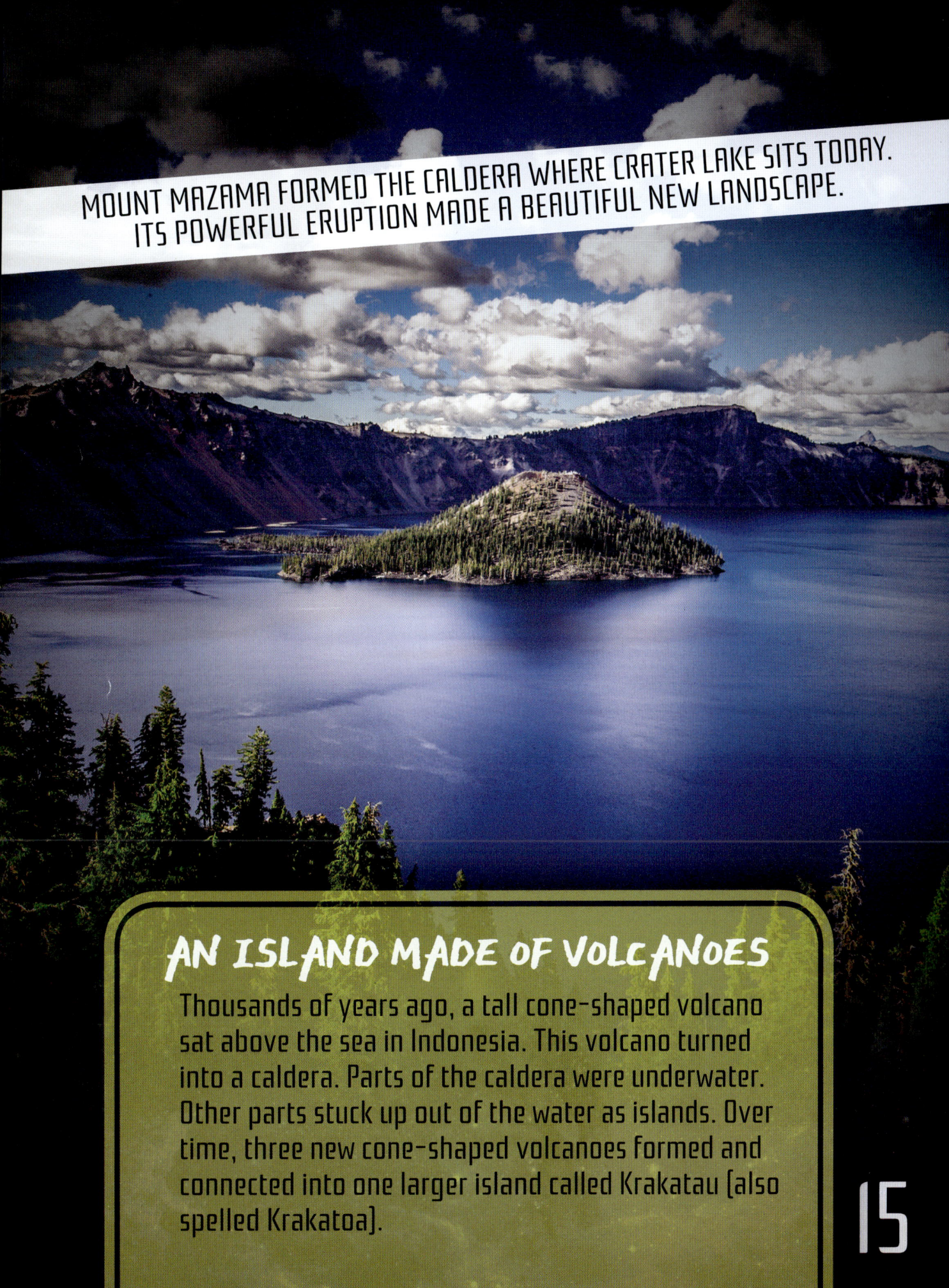

AN ISLAND MADE OF VOLCANOES

Thousands of years ago, a tall cone-shaped volcano sat above the sea in Indonesia. This volcano turned into a caldera. Parts of the caldera were underwater. Other parts stuck up out of the water as islands. Over time, three new cone-shaped volcanoes formed and connected into one larger island called Krakatau (also spelled Krakatoa).

KRAKATAU ERUPTS

Two tectonic plates meet right underneath Krakatau island. There are lots of earthquakes and volcanic eruptions in the area. Krakatau's 1883 eruptions were some of the most harmful in history. These explosive eruptions went on for months. The worst caused **tsunamis**. Though people didn't live on Krakatau island, the biggest tsunami killed 36,000 people on nearby islands.

The strongest eruption threw 5 cubic miles (21 cubic km) of rock into the air. Big chunks of pumice, a volcanic rock that floats, got in the way of ships! Ash from the eruption made the sky dark for two and a half days.

MOST OF ANAK KRAKATAU COLLAPSED IN 2018. THIS CAUSED A TSUNAMI THAT KILLED HUNDREDS OF PEOPLE.

KRAKATAU'S EXPLOSIVE CHILD

Anak Krakatau formed in 1930. It rose out of the water where Krakatau used to be. Its name means "Child of Krakatau." Anak Krakatau goes through times of constant eruptions. Some of these eruptions make lightning in the sky. They also shoot out balls of lava! These beautiful explosions are called Strombolian eruptions.

SUBMARINE VOLCANOES

Many volcanoes are under the water, but they can still erupt! These are called submarine volcanoes. Seamounts are large mountain volcanoes underwater. They're at least 3,300 feet (1,006 m) above the floor of the sea. Scientists think there are more than 20,000 seamounts in Earth's oceans. Seamounts can form chains of 10 to 100 volcanoes.

Small submarine volcanoes are known as sea knolls. Knoll is another word for a hill. Submarine volcanoes with flat tops are called guyots. These were likely once island volcanoes that sank underwater. They were worn flat over time. Some are covered in coral.

A LOOK AT LŌʻIHI

Map labels: Pacific Ocean, Hawaiian Islands, Pacific Ocean, Hawaii, Lōʻihi

LŌʻIHI IS LOCATED ABOUT 19 MILES (30.6 KM) SOUTHEAST OFF THE MAIN ISLAND OF HAWAII.

LŌʻIHI

One famous seamount is Lōʻihi. It's the youngest volcano in the Hawaiian chain. Earthquakes hit under this volcano in the 1970s, and again in 1996. Scientists used a special research submarine to look at Lōʻihi after the 1996 earthquakes. They found that a new crater had formed.

SHIELD VOLCANOES

Shield volcanoes are shaped like domes, or half of a ball. The top is usually a flat caldera. These volcanoes are formed mainly from basaltic lava, a type of lava that flows easily during eruptions. Smaller shield volcanoes are built by constant lava flows. Bigger shield volcanoes take about 1 million years to form. They are the result of many thousands of flowing lava eruptions. Since the lava flows so easily and doesn't pile up, shield volcanoes tend to have very gentle slopes.

Most shield volcano eruptions aren't very explosive. However, if water gets into a shield volcano's vent, it can cause quite a powerful eruption.

MAUNA LOA LAST ERUPTED IN 1984. THIS ERUPTION LASTED 22 DAYS!

ONE BIG VOLCANO

Mauna Loa is a shield volcano in Hawaii. It's the largest active volcano on Earth! Mauna Loa means "long mountain." It covers around half of the Island of Hawaii. It's 55,700 feet (16,977 m) high from its base. It's also one of the most active volcanoes known today. It's erupted 33 times since 1843.

LAVA DOMES

Very thick lava sometimes forms lava domes. Lava domes are round on top. The lava is sometimes squeezed up through a volcano's vent like toothpaste through a tube. The lava is too thick to flow away easily, so it balls up over the vent. Lava domes can form inside the calderas of volcanoes.

A lava dome's outside layer hardens when it cools. As more lava flows from the vent, the outside layer breaks up into small pieces and falls. This makes room for the new layer underneath. Lava domes can form from explosions or from lava leaking more slowly.

THE LASSEN PEAK DOME FORMED ABOUT 27,000 YEARS AGO! TODAY, IT'S PROTECTED AS THE LASSEN VOLCANIC NATIONAL PARK.

LAVA CHAOS!

Northern California is home to one of the largest volcanic domes in the world—the upper part of Lassen Peak. It's more than 2,000 feet (610 m) tall and 2 miles (3.2 km) wide! The Chaos Crags are a whole row of lava domes near the Lassen Peak. A crag is a high and steep area of rock.

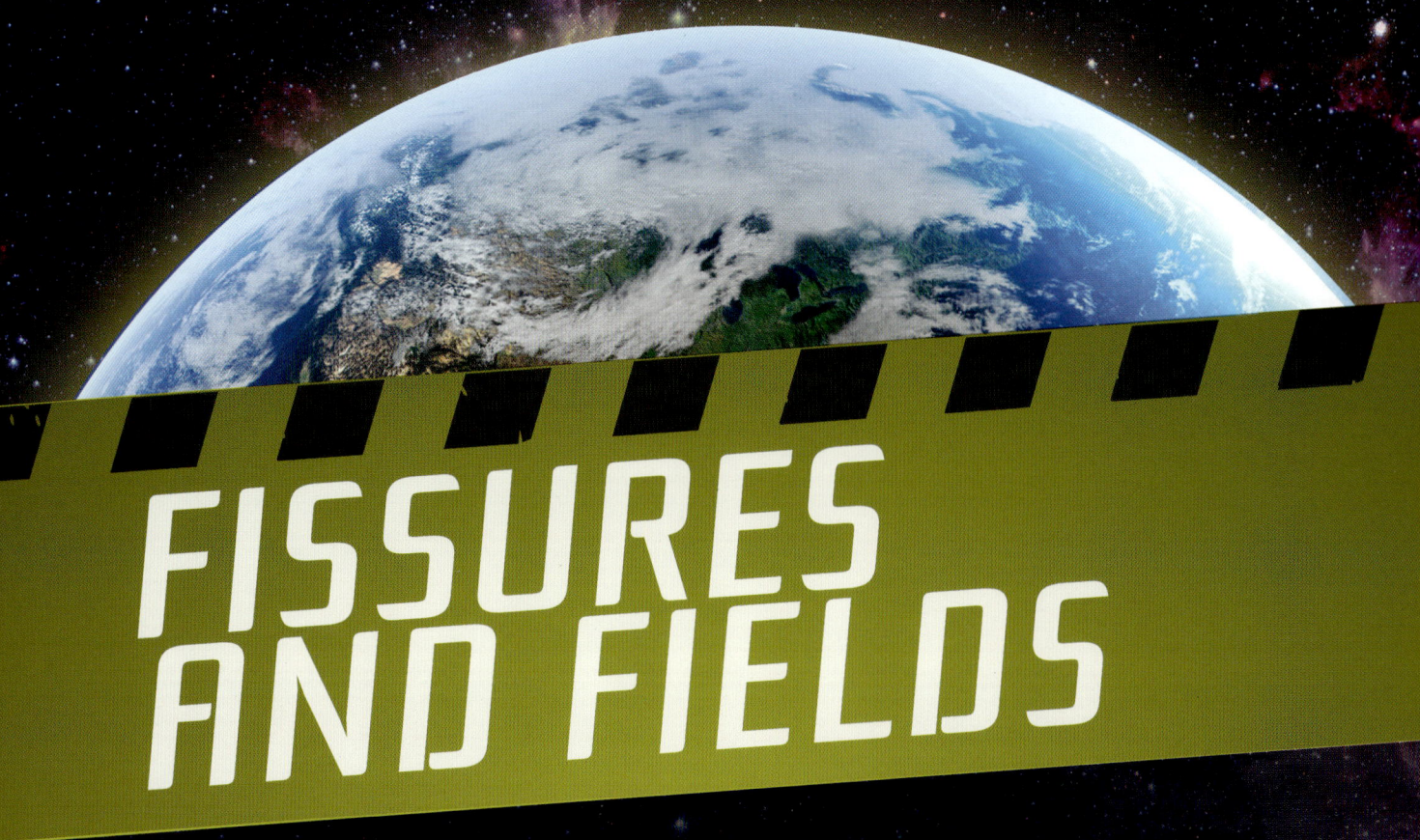

FISSURES AND FIELDS

Some volcanic vents are long cracks in rock. They're called fissures. These are only a few feet wide, but they can be miles long. Fissures usually form in the ground or bottom of the ocean. This can make them hard to find. The fissure vents in some Hawaiian volcanoes shoot up walls of lava. Most eruptions from fissures aren't explosive. But sometimes, they're very powerful.

One of the worst eruptions ever came from the Laki fissure and Grímsvötn volcano in Iceland in 1783. The eruption caused illnesses and killed animals and plants. This led to famines that killed thousands of people.

ASTRONAUTS HAVE PRACTICED MOONWALKING IN ICELAND, INCLUDING AT THE ELDHRAUN LAVA FIELD. SOME OF THE ROCKS, CRATERS, AND OTHER FEATURES FOUND HERE ARE THOUGHT TO BE SIMILAR TO THOSE ON THE MOON.

A LUSH LAVA FIELD

A lava field is an area of land that is covered in a lava flow. The flow cools into a flat, hard surface. The 1783 eruption in Iceland made the Eldhraun lava field. It's 218 square miles (565 sq km)! Today, the Eldhraun lava field is covered in lush, or healthy, moss.

SUPERVOLCANOES

The most powerful volcanoes are commonly called supervolcanoes. They sit on top of huge pools of magma. The magma builds up lots of pressure. Then, it explodes! Supervolcanoes erupt more than 240 cubic miles (1,000 cu km) of lava and tephra. These eruptions form huge calderas.

Supervolcanic eruptions, sometimes called supereruptions, can change the climate of the whole planet. Ash and gases from the eruption can cool Earth.

Luckily, supervolcanic eruptions are very rare. The most recent supervolcanic eruption was Taupo in New Zealand. It erupted 22,600 years ago.

YELLOWSTONE'S MANY **HYDROTHERMAL** FEATURES ARE SIGNS OF THE SUPERVOLCANO BELOW THE PARK'S SURFACE.

GEYSERS AND HOT SPRINGS

Yellowstone National Park in the United States is a supervolcano, and it's already active! Magma moving beneath the park causes thousands of earthquakes each year. The park also releases heat from magma through geysers and hot springs. Geysers are jets of hot water. They shoot out of vents in the earth. Hot springs are pools of very hot water.

RECENT ERUPTIONS

About 50 to 70 volcanoes erupt every year. The Kīlauea volcano eruption in 2018 was one of the worst in Hawaii's history. It released enough lava to fill about 320,000 Olympic swimming pools! The volcano formed a caldera.

In 2019, the Whakaari volcano in New Zealand erupted. It's better known as White Island. As of January 2020, at least 20 people had died from the eruption.

Earth's surface is always changing. As time goes on, there will be more volcanic eruptions. Volcanologists have the important job of watching for signs of these eruptions so they can warn people to clear the surrounding areas.

TENS OF THOUSANDS OF EARTHQUAKES HIT THE KĪLAUEA CALDERA AFTER THE ERUPTION.

YELLOWSTONE ERUPTIONS

There have already been at least three supervolcanic eruptions at Yellowstone. Scientists think these eruptions were 1,000 times the size of the Mount Saint Helens eruption in 1980. Yellowstone will likely erupt again someday, but scientists guess it won't happen for thousands of years or more.

GLOSSARY

collapse: to fall down or cave in

debris: pieces left when something is destroyed

earthquake: a shaking of the ground caused by the movement of Earth's crust

famine: a situation where many people don't have enough food

greenhouse effect: the process in which gases in Earth's atmosphere trap the sun's heat and heat Earth

hydrothermal: having to do with hot water, especially mixed with minerals from cooling magma

landslide: the sudden movement of rocks and dirt down a hill or mountain

predict: to tell or guess what will happen in the future

satellite: an object that circles Earth in order to collect and send information or aid in communication

tsunami: a huge wave of water created by an underwater earthquake or volcano

FOR MORE INFORMATION

BOOKS

Klatte, Kathleen A. *Reefs and Volcanoes: How Earth's Atolls Formed.* New York, NY: PowerKids Press, 2020.

Nargi, Lela. *Volcanoes.* Washington, DC: National Geographic Children's Books, 2018.

Rose, Simon. *Amazing Volcanoes Around the World.* North Mankato, MN: Capstone Press, 2019.

WEBSITES

17 Explosive Volcano Facts
www.kids.nationalgeographic.com/explore/science/volcano/
Learn more about volcanoes here!

What Is a Volcano?
www.dkfindout.com/us/earth/volcanoes/what-is-volcano/
Explore this interactive site to learn more about volcanoes!

Publisher's note to educators and parents: Our editors have carefully reviewed these websites to ensure that they are suitable for students. Many websites change frequently, however, and we cannot guarantee that a site's future contents will continue to meet our high standards of quality and educational value. Be advised that students should be closely supervised whenever they access the internet.

INDEX

ash 4, 8, 16, 28
basalt 20
caldera 14, 15, 20, 22, 26, 28, 29
Crater Lake 14, 15
Eldhraun lava field 25
fissures 24
gas 4, 6, 8, 9, 26
guyots 18
Hawaii 19, 21, 24, 28
Kīlauea 28, 29
Krakatau (Krakatoa) 15, 16, 17
lahar 8, 9, 12
Lassen Peak 23
lava 4, 8, 10, 11, 17, 20, 22, 23, 24, 25, 26, 28
lava domes 22, 23

Lōʻihi 19
magma 4, 6, 14, 26, 27
Mauna Loa 21
Mount Saint Helens 12, 13, 29
Mount Vesuvius 11
Nevado del Ruiz 9
pyroclastic flows 8, 11
Ring of Fire 5
seamount 18, 19
stratovolcanoes 10, 11, 12
supervolcanoes 26, 27
Taupo 26
volcanologist 6, 7, 28
White Island 28
Yellowstone National Park 27, 29